Fashioning Value — Undressing Ornament

A critical study of fashion as a system of value production, through the paradigmatic changes of ornament

Femke de Vries

Index

7 Part 0.
An Introduction

11 Part 1.
The Designer as Ornamentor

15 Part 2.
Ornament and Obsolescence

25 Part 3.
Ornament as Commodity

35 Part 4.
Ornamenting the Inner- Instead of the Outer Self

41 Part 5.
Fashioning the Mind

49 Part 6.
Today's Ornament: a Fleeting State of Mind

57 Part 7.
Clothes as Souvenirs

67 Part 8.
The User as Ornamentor

77 Part 9.
To Conclude, for Now

Undressing Ornament

Fas
Valı
Und.
ɔrna.
shic
ıe

Part 0.
An Introduction

Ornament and its economic and social implications are often referred to within design and architecture; Adolf Loos and Hal Foster in particular have made striking statements on this subject. In *Ornament and Crime* Adolf Loos expresses a critical view on the effect of overabundance and dominance of ornament during the Art Nouveau period.[✦] In *Design and Crime* Hal Foster, elaborating on Loos's work, concentrates on total design, designing both the environment and the 'person' living in it, and how it would end the subject's potential.[❁]

Considering their arguments in a contemporary context reveals the predominance of a specific form of ornament that has a strong impact on today's makers and users in a design culture driven by fashion.

During my Bachelor of Fashion Design studies I was trained as a fashion designer. I learned how to decorate objects in a literal sense: to add ornamentation to basic everyday clothing items in order to adjust their look. The emphasis was placed on how to design or ornament a T-shirt, a pair of trousers, a sweater, a dress, etcetera. To clarify, I would like to define 'design' in this example as being mainly concerned with the decoration or ornamentation of clothing items. We are all familiar with the basic shapes of everyday garments. By constantly changing the ornamentation of these basic shapes – not just in the sense of a print, but also by changing color, detail, cut and material – new T-shirts, dresses, etcetera are put on the market every season.

✦ LOOS, ADOLF. (1908) *Ornament and Crime*. [Online] Available from http://www2.gwu.edu/~art/Tempo-

❁ FOSTER, HAL. (2002) *Design and Crime, And Other Diatribes*, London/ New York: Verso

However, it is important to recognize the development of another form of ornament, which shares the characteristics of literal ornamentation but, today, has an even stronger effect on makers, users and objects than the literal ornament. This ornament takes the form of commercially constructed values in which brands, advertising, fashion and experience design play a key role. Examples of such values can be happiness, fun, authenticity, etcetera. Advanced with great determination through branding, this value-ornament has acquired a dominant position in today's consumer society.

During my Master of Fashion Strategy I was introduced to the world of these constructed values: fashion (brand) strategies and identities. Besides designing clothes, I studied the development of symbolic ornaments and the various strategies to communicate them.

Working on my graduation project, I had a conversation with an expert in branding and strategy from a successful commercial fashion trend forecasting company. When I explained to him that I wanted to address these symbolic values in my work – and even to investigate if it were possible to strip fashion objects of these values entirely – his reaction was rather disapproving. He believed that my working principle was the exact opposite of what the fashion industry is trying to achieve, which is all about creating 'added value'.

It is exactly this 'added value' – such an elusive, almost magical power – as the essence of fashion that intrigues me. Its pervasiveness and strong economic function provoke numerous questions concerning the manner of its production, the scope and nature of the roles it fulfills and the way this value is used or consumed. Comparing this symbolic ornament to the literal ornament it becomes clear that added value, in fashion, clearly references the way literal ornament is described in the design discourse. Descriptions of the literal ornament refer to an increase of temporality; the influence on the user (diminishing personal space); the dominant position of the maker; and the underlying economic and social motivations and effects. Due to the layered character of ornament and the way it is referenced in various discourses, using its definition and paradigmatic changes as a starting point offered the opportunity to research the different stakeholders within today's fashion system from various perspectives. By approaching ornament from a critical viewpoint, this text maps the intangible elements of fashion as a system of value production, offering insights into today's design process and future scenarios.

In short, through references to ornament this text explores six main areas:

. The order of the design process and its effect on what defines the maker;
. The form of the ornament evolving into a contemporary intangible value ornament that shifts from being an addition to representing the essence, impacting the role of the consumer, the designer and the material object;
. The economic and commercial context of planned obsolescence through changes in value-related perception with the use of branding and storytelling;
. The intrinsic character of ornament focusing on feelings that fits seamlessly with today's experience economy in which self-design becomes a creed;

- The effect today's ornament can have on the role of the material object in fashion, acting merely as a souvenir;
- The effect of today's ornament on the role of the user in relation to the maker and vice versa, culminating in the realization that today's ornament, in spite of being characterized by commercially constructed feelings and fantasies, and in spite of its determined and dominant approach, offers possible new scenarios for both the user and the maker.

Part 1.
The Designer as Ornamentor

Ornament: the first thought that comes to mind is that it is a visible addition to the surface of an object, an addition that does not have any influence on the object's practical function. It can, however, have a connection to this function, for example when a seam is elongated with a striking color.

In his book *The Rise of Design: Design and Domestic Interior in Eighteenth-Century England*[**] Charles Saumarez Smith describes how ornamentation in architecture was originally considered a separate element that could be added to existing interior and exterior elements such as walls, ceilings, doors etcetera. He also explains that in England, for the largest part of the 17th century, a master engineer developed buildings and only after these were built various decorators were invited to decorate the interiors according to their personal viewpoint or taste. These decorations were of no additional practical value to the building and were chosen on the basis of stylebooks that contained endless lists of ornaments that could be applied quite randomly. These books never showed interiors in their entirety; only particular elements for particular parts of the interior. It was around 1650, that the tasks of a master engineer and a decorator would slowly be combined so that construction and ornamentation became synchronized in a preconceived building plan. This change in the building process is the first important step towards design, according to Saumarez Smith.

** SAUMAREZ SMITH, CHARLES. (1993) *The Rise of Design: Design and Domestic Interior in Eight-*

Architect and theorist Adolf Loos (1870-1933) gave considerable thought to the subject of this interweaving of tasks. In his text *Ornament and Crime*

Fig. 1

Zippers, belts, and ties are prohibited. These items as well as pockets on shirts are considered ornamental and frivolous.

(1908)* he conjures up the cobbler who makes and decorates his shoes. Loos contemplates the option of asking him if the decoration could be omitted, leaving a shoe in its 'purest' form – a question that implies that the cobbler's job could be split in two: a shoe 'builder' and a shoe 'decorator'. Loos would like to request his cobbler to skip the decoration because he is convinced that decoration, or ornamentation, will cause a product to become obsolete sooner and therefore enforce the consumption of new products. According to Loos another consequence of the ornamentation of objects is an increase in labor and material and a decrease of material quality. Loos's vision was quite radical for his time considering that Art Nouveau – the leading art movement at the time when he wrote *Ornament and Crime* – was identified by an abundance of ornamentation. These ornaments did not have any practical value to the user, and thus could be, according to Loos, experienced as an imposed taste. Loos's statement on the reduction of ornament was also inherently socio-political. When he asks the cobbler (who would ornament the bare product according to his own taste, or to the taste preferred by, for example, a ruling elite) *not* to impose this taste upon the user, he addresses and questions the hierarchy between maker and user. While Loos is an outspoken critic of the uninvited interweaving of making an object and decorating it, Saumarez Smith considers this same interweaving of tasks into a preconceived plan as the first important step towards 'design'. Thus, the role of the designer is characterized by a working process in which 'building' and ornamentation (according to the maker's taste or the tastes of a ruling elite) is combined in a pre-conceived plan. This stresses the difference between, for example, a dressmaker and a fashion designer.

* LOOS, ADOLF. (1908) *Ornament and Crime*. [Online]. Available from http://www2.gwu.edu/~art/Tempo-

However, the preconceived plan implemented by today's designers differs in an essential way from the example of the cobbler who integrates 'building' and 'ornamentation'. While the majority of fashion designers today synthesize the ornamentation and 'building' of a piece of clothing in a preconceived plan, they skip the task of the actual making: the technical side of production. The construction of the pieces of clothing is outsourced to factories or dressmakers and tailors. As such, today's designers are mainly concerned with ornament or, in Loos's conception, with imposing taste. Dividing the designer's work once more into two separate tasks, with a focus on ornament, raises the question: could the contemporary (fashion) designer more accurately be described as an ornamentor? This takes us back to the role of the ornamentor in 17th-century 'building' in England, where the ornamentor's only task was to decorate the already built interior. The main difference today is that 'building' actually starts with ornament, which leads to another question; what is the effect of this focus on ornament?

Part 2.
Ornament and Obsolescence

According to Loos, ornament plays an important role in the marketing of products people don't actually need. For one thing, ornament as an addition or 'dressing' opens up the possibility to change the appearance of a product in a quick and simple manner. With every change, whether enriching or masking aspects of the original object, a 'new' and therefore desirable version is created. This means that ornament plays a central role in the dynamic of change that is characteristic of the past two centuries in which industrialization set in motion a continuous cycle of production and consumption of commodities leading to the rise of modernity, capitalism and fashion as we know it today. This dynamic of change affected the citizen as a consumer and as a worker. Loos writes that if all objects would last as long as materially possible, the consumer would pay a price that would generate more money for the producer and thus the possibility of reducing his working hours.

> *If all objects would last aesthetically as long as they do physically, the consumer could pay a price for them that would enable the worker to earn more money and work shorter hours. For an object I am sure I can use to its full extent I willingly pay four times as much as for one that is inferior in form or material. I happily pay forty kronen for my boots, although in a different shop I could get boots for ten kronen.*°

° LOOS, ADOLF. (1908) Ornament and Crime. [Online]. Availa ble from http://www2.gwu.edu/~art/Tempo-

Loos's vision of the future in relation to the 'worker' links to the ideas of John Maynard Keynes.※ In the book *How Much is Enough?*⁺ Robert and Edward Skidelsky discuss Keynes' projection that technological developments will lead to reduced working hours and a more equal division of labor by around 2030. The Skidelskys give strong reasons to doubt this prophecy to ever become a reality. As the title of their book suggests, the Skidelskys pose the question: when do we have enough? This question brings together the 'worker' and the consumer, as we all are, to some extent, both.◆

A radical change in regard to demand, supply and market saturation took place in the United States of America at the beginning of the 20th century. Due to advances in technology and creative science the industrial productivity increased tremendously, giving rise to a fear of market saturation. The essential economic problem became one of organizing buyers rather than stimulating producers. One of the solutions was planned obsolescence×: a strategy used to adjust products in such a manner that they become obsolete sooner, making way for new products to be introduced and stimulating their sales. The embedding of obsolescence can be achieved by introducing functional elements with a limited lifespan, like non-replaceable batteries, or objects with singular functions that are inadaptable. It can, however, also be accomplished by changing the perception of the surface appearance of a commodity. This is commonly referred to as style obsolescence. It is this style obsolescence that shows strong parallels with ornament. Loos's remarks on ornament as a means to change the surface appearance and its capacity to reduce an object's lifespan clearly illustrate how ornament can be understood as a tool of planned obsolescence.

Economic Possibilities for our Grandchildren. [Online] New York: W.W. Norton & Co. Available from http://www.econ.yale.edu/smith/econ116a/keynes1.

(Scanned from John Maynard Keynes, Essays in Persuasion, New York: W.W. Norton & Co., 1963, pp. 358-373.)

EDWARD. (2012) *Hoeveel is Genoeg? Geld en het verlangen naar een goed leven.* (*How Much is Enough? Money and the Good Life*). Amsterdam:

Fig. 2

"In contrast to western fluidity and rapid change, the epic socialist master narrative expressed itself through a slow flow of time."

◆ The merging of these two roles relates to Hannah Arendt when she mentions workers that earned enough money to

but now also on the 'superfluous') symbolizing a crucial change in the relation between labor and consump- tion that capitalism is based upon.

Human Condition [Online] Available from http://sduk.us/afterwork/arendt_the_human_condition.pdf [Accessed on 09/01/2015]

× LONDON, BERNARD. (1932) *Ending the Depression Trough Planned Obsolescence.* [Online] Available from

Fig. 3

Here we have always associated movement with life and the passage of time, but from my experience within the forest near Mont Royal I know that all motion leads inevitably to death, and that time is its servant.

He simply didn't know
how he should act with
a dead man beside him.
The flow of time is so
different for the dead
and the living.

> *Changes of ornament lead to a premature devaluation of the labour product. (…) This is well known to the ornamentalist, and Austrian ornamentalists are trying to make the best of this shortcoming. They say; 'We prefer a consumer who has a set of furniture that becomes intolerable to him after ten years, and who is consequently forced to refurnish every ten years, to one who only buys an object when the old one is worn out. Industry demands this. Millions are employed as a result of the quick change.*◈

The parallels between the effect of ornament and the goal of style obsolescence become apparent: ornament makes 'products' go out of style – even if this was never the goal of adding ornamentation. Style obsolescence is based on the predetermined idea to cause things to go out of style, which can be achieved through ornamentation.

Considering that style obsolescence can manifest itself as the adjustment of the surface appearance of a commodity, it can directly be linked to the fashion industry and the seasonal changes of clothes by changing looks and styles through literal 'material' ornamentation: a new length, a new color, a new print, etcetera. However, referring to the 1920s and 1930s (when Bernard London wrote *Ending the Depression Through Planned Obsolescence*), the economic situation and developments in psychological science of the time created the opportunity for another interesting form of ornamentation to emerge in relation to obsolescence. This form of ornamentation gives a completely new dimension to the change of the surface appearance of a commodity.

Crime. [Online] Available from http:// www2.gwu.edu/~art/Temporary_ … on 10/10/2007]

To introduce this new form it is useful to refer to Vance Packard's *The Waste Makers** (1960). Vance Packard divided planned obsolescence into two subcategories: one of desirability and one of function. For obsolescence of desirability he also used the term 'psychological obsolescence' which referred to marketers attempt to 'wear a product in the owner's mind'.✻

Vance Packard used the term psychological obsolescence in the 1960s, but four decades earlier, Sigmund Freud's nephew Edward Bernays had already pioneered a way of manipulating the masses to buy new products before the old products were broken or 'worn out' by directing his attention to 'the owner's mind'. Bernays coined the term Public Relations for this approach, which had emerged from propaganda. Drawing on his uncle's theories of psychoanalysis, he believed there had to be a change in mentality leading to a culture driven by 'desire' rather than by 'need': "Man's desire must overshadow his needs".⅄ He instilled this desire not by advertising the practical characteristics of a product, but by creating symbolic value that could be added to the product in order to change the way it was perceived by the public. Using this approach he succeeded, for example, to make smoking a socially acceptable habit for women. To accomplish this, Bernays arranged a public event where beautiful women would be seen smoking cigarettes. Press images of the event were then published alongside the powerful slogan "torches of freedom".* In this way, using cultural symbols, conventions and understandings, the product was given a new connotation of desirability. Promoting products not as something the consumer needs but as something that would make the con-

* PACKARD, VANCE. (1960) *The Waste Makers*. United States: Vance Packard Inc. (first edition)

✻ Ibid.

⅄ CURTIS, ADAM. (2002) *The Century* [Online video]. Available from http://sophistryandillusion.com/videos/Adam-Curtis/The+Century+of+the+-

* Machines%29.flv.php. Accessed on 19/11/2013]

sumer happy – in this case through a sense of emancipation – was a fairly new phenomenon. Before Bernays, shoes, stockings, cars, etcetera were mainly advertised by emphasizing their function and their durability: the appraisal of practical characteristics. Bernays discovered that to stimulate consumerism, it wasn't necessary to focus on practical characteristics or changing the product itself, but rather to change the way the product was perceived, the value-related perception.

The symbolic added value championed by Bernays can be defined as an adjustment of the surface appearance of the product by adding a 'style', in this case a certain value, idea or meaning. Although this idea or value is intangible, its characteristics clearly refer to the traditional notion of the 'literal' ornament: the 'style' or ornament Bernays adds does not aim to improve the product's functional characteristics; it requires no technical knowledge from the maker about the material product it will be added to; and it can be developed separately from the product and added to it later. Just like the literal ornament, this form of style can be seen as a standalone element that can be added as a 'dressing', a covering layer. It lacks practical functionality but enriches – and sometimes masks – the bare product with the purpose of seducing the consumer to obtain the 'new' while simultaneously making sure the 'old' goes 'out of style'. From this perspective, the symbolic value developed and added by Bernays can be considered an ornament: a commercially constructed value-ornament. Key to this definition is the fact that Bernays developed a way to formulate and communicate a new kind of commercial ornament that transformed the understanding of style from merely 'a look' into an element of perceived worth and value.

Although a change in appearance of an object through literal ornamentation already evokes a perception of 'newness' and its stimulating effect on consumption, the ornamentation through adding symbolic value is one of today's most effective tools to create obsolescence of desirability or psychological obsolescence. Firstly because it directly addresses the owner's mind by using cultural symbols, conventions and understandings, and secondly because the symbolic value-ornament that is key to this approach effects only the intangible surface appearance and therefore exists independently from any practical materialistic character of the product. Because the value-ornament doesn't require any innovation of materials, production modes or functionalities it facilitates an easy production of the 'new'. It therefore stimulates a smooth introduction of objects into the fashion system. While clearly related to fashion, which is mostly associated with clothing, this form of changing 'style' or surface appearance also occurs in interior design, transport, technology, education, healthcare, etcetera.

The symbolic value-ornament developed by Bernays, which focused on value-related perception, today would be referred to as branding. This approach played a key role in the creation of a system built on desirability rather than need, and has come to occupy a central role in the consumer society and a capitalist system striving for constant change.

Designers, in fashion as well as in other fields, today work with both visible, material ornaments and symbolic ornament, often in the form of values wrapped in 'stories'. Both forms of ornament offer the possibility to change the surface appearance or 'style'. But it is the intangible symbolic value–ornament that most effectively enhances the desire for the new by addressing the value related perception: the owner's mind. It functions as a powerful and fast tool for creating psychological obsolescence and is an accelerant in the continued renewal and consumption of products, which, in turn, keeps the worker working in order to afford these products. Therefore this symbolic ornament, as an addition to the literal ornament, is responsible for indefinitely delaying the projected liberation of the worker proposed by Loos and Keynes.

Part 3.
Ornament as Commodity

The post-industrial society◈ brought forth the information society. Due to a strong emphasis on communication, this transition caused a shift in focus from the material object to intangible values. Luca Marchetti addresses this in the article *From the object to the invisible: Retail experience within space, fashion and body*:

> *Although objects have always had a meaning that transcends their functional dimension (for instance, ritual values), the recent interest in the thin body of artefacts seems to indicate that this issue is particularly relevant in our information-based society, in which the invisible is as important as the tangible – if not more.*✚

The relevance of this statement within contemporary design is underscored in the 99th edition (Jul/Aug 2014) of Frame magazine, which contains an insert booklet called *Product and Form: The Shape of 2014 and Beyond.* This supplement is introduced explaining that Frame pauses to analyze products and form from inside out in the afterglow of the yearly Milan furniture fair Salone del Mobile, described as the number-one event on almost every design professional's calendar. The introduction concludes with the following sentence summarizing the fair in short: "Never before have stories behind products been so important." *

◈ The postindustrial society is marked by a transition from a manufac- turing-based economy focused on

manufactures produce goods directly. There is an increased valuation of knowledge, information and ideas

the Object to the Invisible: Retail Experience within Space, Fashion and Body. In: Brand, Jan Teunissen

* FRAME. (2014) Product and Form *Frame* 99. (Jul/Aug 2014). p. 130.

The importance of the intangible values or symbolic ornamentation, usually wrapped in stories, brand and designer identities, is evident not just from the importance attributed to these ornaments, but from the things that are considered to be less important as well. For example: one of fourteen tips given by fashion designer Tom Ford to young designers in the crowd at the 2013 CFDA/ Vogue Fashion Fund Awards was: "Remember that our customers do not need our clothes." ◗ This statement can be interpreted in a number of ways. Firstly, with this statement, Ford could be suggesting that owning designer clothes is not a necessity. Secondly and more importantly Ford, highly competent in fashion branding, is pointing out that today, clothes, as material objects, are not what really matter within fashion and consumer society. The statement implies that customers may not *need* the clothes themselves but do *desire* something else; their symbolic value. Ford reminds his audience that designers need to address this desire for value in order to sell clothes.

The traditional view holds that (fashion) designers design clothes and that the piece of clothing as an object of use – whether to protect or to express oneself – is the starting point in the process of development and purchase. To understand the present-day design process it is useful to look at the process of ornamentation as described by Franz Sales Meyer at the end of the 19th century. In his *Handbook of Ornament* he explains the process of ornamenting as follows: "When merely drawn on paper, &c., and unapplied – a foliated element is considered in the abstract as "Ornament". When applied to beautify an object – it becomes an "element of decoration". The term decoration signifies the art or process of applying the various elements to beautify objects."※

FRANK, JULIA. (2013) *Tom Ford's 14 Tips on Building a Fashion Brand.* [online] 14th November 2013. Available from: *Vogue.com* http://www.vogue.com.au/fashion/news/tom+fords+14+tips+on+building+a+fashion+brand, 28189. [Accessed in May 2014]

SALES MEYER, FRANZ. (2013) *Handbook of Ornament, 3003 illustrations.* First edition: 1957. New York: Dover Publications. p. VII.

Clearly, the reality of today's design process is rather more complex than an ornamentor who creates an ornament, a builder who builds the material object and a decorator who applies the ornament to the object. Meyer's description offers the opportunity to bring today's most common design process into view. The ornamentor (sometimes referred to as creative director■) – who has first thought out the story, the invisible symbolic values or ornaments – collaborates with a 'builder' (a dressmaker or factory for example) who helps him manufacture the material product that carries these values and functions as a scaffolding. In the case of the symbolic ornament, the next step: to apply ornament to the built object, or turn ornament into decoration, is, primarily a task for the advertiser, who uses various media to make sure the intangible ornament adheres to the material object. This process of bringing ornament and object together – decoration – is in most cases outsourced, just like the 'building' of the material product itself.

> *(…) Nike doesn't actually own any machines or equipment at all. The company only develops footwear concepts and designs, and, in a sense, even the "philosophy" of a certain product. All other production (including the creative stage of advertising and marketing) is handled by partner companies and license holders.*★

The focus of designers on ornament – symbolic value embodied in stories, brand and designer identities – is closely linked to the outsourcing or division of tasks, which underlines the role of today's designer as ornamentor. Frame Magazine (2014) describes this redefinition of the role of the designer

■ "As creative director of Burberry, Fabien Baron was closely involved in many aspects of the British brand's rebrand by not only modernising the logo (…), but by creating an advertising campaign before there was any new product to advertise." BLANCHARD.

Hanka van der with Brand, Jan. (eds.) *Couture Graphique*. Houten: Uitgeverij Terra Lannoo bv.

★ Beyond Materiality and Immateriality. In *e-flux journal. Are You Working Too Much? Post Fordism, Precarity, and the Labor of Art.* Sternberg Press.

and ornament within the design process by printing the following statement on its cover: “Speak up, designers must be storytellers.”*

Where Bernays’ symbolic ornament was still added to existing products just like the literal ornament, today’s value-ornament is the starting point in the design process. It is the essence of design and exceeds utility value. Although craftsmanship and hands-on materialism currently enjoy increased popularity, apparently paying more attention to the materialistic object and in some cases actually improving ‘products’, in a commercial context this emphasis mainly derives from a strong symbolic value-ornament: authenticity.

This focus on meaning instead of practical utility value and on the designer as ornamentor brings about a transformation of the role and character of the material product. Subordinate to the value-ornament, it now only functions as a carrier of meaning and, as a result, the actual material product becomes easily interchangeable with other products. This, in turn, allows a designer or fashion brand to not only create clothes but also make-up, perfume, shoes, sunglasses, cars, furniture, etcetera, without the necessity of knowledge of the product’s material and/or functional characteristics. Again quoting Frame Magazine and its reflection on the ‘number one furniture fair’: “Anything goes, based on the story.”▼

Frame 99. (Jul/Aug 2014). p. cover.

Form Survey. *Frame 99*. (Jul/Aug 2014). p. 147. An answer from Mario Minale, from design studio Minale-

forms of 2014.

Fig. 5

COATS COAT COAT STORE AS NOVEL SALES SCHEME

OVERSTOCKED with a large supply of men's spring and winter coats, a clothier in Copenhagen, Denmark, adopted a unique sales scheme. He erected a scaffolding around his store building and completely covered it from roof to sidewalk with more than a thousand overcoats. The novel display attracted prospective customers in such droves that police were summoned. Although the police ordered the proprietor to remove the display, he succeeded in selling all the overcoats.

In this scenario, where the material object exists primarily as a carrier, the object's main function is to make the symbolic ornament obtainable, useable and 'consumable'. Philip Knight, the Chairman of the Board of Directors of Nike makes clear that, for Nike, the product is not the essence but has become an interchangeable instrument to accomplish a goal. Explaining that Nike, for a long period of time, saw itself as a production-oriented company but now considers the marketing of products to be its main task, he says that Nike is a marketing-oriented company and that the product is its most important marketing tool.* The product is a tool, not the goal. The goal is creating, presenting, and selling the Nike experience and identity. The material product only makes sure this intangible ornament can be carried around by the consumer, so that we can relate to it in daily life. Especially in clothing, as light material objects, the symbolic value is easily carried around as it is worn close to the body.

With Public Relations, Edward Bernays successfully introduced the symbolic ornament that has now become the essence of the commodity. Bernays' ornament, as a loose element that could be added later in the process, evolved into a contemporary value-ornament that exists as the core, a stand-alone element to which almost any object can be adhered.

If ornament has become the main motivation in a commodity's production and consumption, it is possible to conclude that ornament has not just become the essence of the commodity, but has *become* the commodity. The actual material object has thus become what the ornament once was: an addition.

* KLEIN, NAOMI. (2011) *No Logo: De strijd tegen de dwang van de wereldmerken (No Logo: Taking Aim at the Brand Bullies.* First edition published in 2000). Rotterdam: Lemniscaat. p.51.

Fig. 6

Fig. 7

Still, inside here, this is what I think: if we reverse the outer shell and the essence – in other words, consider the outer shell the essence and the essence only the shell – our lives might be a whole lot easier to understand.

Decoration is no longer applied to an object; it is the object.❤

(…) we see that the neomaterialistic economy is one in which symbols behave like materials.❖

❤ RAME. (2014) Frame Product and Form, in the Mix. *Frame*. 99. (Jul/Aug 2014). p. 145. A quote from Eero and design studio Claesson Koivisto Rune in Stockholm, Sweden.

❖ SIMON, JOSHUA. (2013) *Neomaterialism*, Berlin: Sternberg Press. p. 25.

Part 4.
Ornamenting the Inner-
Instead of the Outer Self

Ornament has made a transition from the tangible to the intangible, has become the starting point in the design process and is the main motivation for the consumer to buy a particular product. In addition to this shift, the intrinsic character of ornament is also subject to change. While it is important to remember that ornaments in the traditional sense continue to exist next to the ornaments falling under the contemporary definition, this new symbolic value-ornament currently has a more dominant presence and has in most cases become the unique selling point.

The industrialization and the accompanying shift from rural to city life contributed strongly to the growing importance of constructed symbolic values and to the developing notions of the individual and the individual's malleability. This had great influence on the character of ornament in relation to the identity of the user. Writing about the growing population in cities at the start of the industrial revolution, Luca Marchetti said: "In the new metropolis of the eighteenth century, the main attraction is represented by those products that create 'refinement', that is to say veritable signs able to communicate the position of he or she who wears them, in a social landscape in constant evolution."✓ In relation to dress these distinctive ornaments became important advertisers of the wearer's position within a social landscape. Georg Simmel writes that in fashion there is a tension between imitation to create a social identity and distinction to create an individual identity.*

✓ MARCHETTI, LUCA. (2009) From the Object to the Invisible: Retail Experience within Space, Fashion José. *Fashion & Imagination*. ArtEZ Press, d'JongeHond, p. 172.

* SIMMEL, GEORG (1904) *Fashion.* [Online] (09/2010). Available from http://sites.middlebury.edu/individu- Simmel.fashion.pdf [Accessed on 15/01/2015]

In the documentary *The Century of The Self* ✖ a fragment is shown of an American saleswoman around 1920, explaining the psychology of dress to the public. Speaking of dressing, the woman states that it is not about communicating one's position, as Luca Marchetti writes in reference to dress in the 18th century, but about expressing one's inner self – which relates to the individual identity mentioned by Simmel. The woman explains that every single person has an interesting character and this character deserves to be shown. She wonders aloud why this is not done very often: why people all dress the same. The woman encourages her audience to express themselves better in the way they dress.❄ From this viewpoint, ornament (both literal and symbolic) can both conceal and communicate distinctions of position or personality. It dresses the person with a layer of ornamentation that communicates certain values by wearing a certain fabric or style for example, or by clearly wearing a particular brand logo. Showing one's position, be it political or social, through ornamentation and expressing ones personality or personal emotional state of mind, nowadays is followed by an interesting step that affects the intrinsic character of ornament and, in the context of Simmel's argument, adds an extra dimension to the tension that defines fashion.

In contemporary Western society there is an all-encompassing emphasis on developing our inner emotional selves. In education and the job market, phrases like "passion" and "personal qualities" are presented as the key to success. Given the fact that the majority of the work force in the Western world is highly educated and is competing in similar areas of expertise, we are told that it is one's personality that can make the difference when applying for a job. The idea that personality is malleable has given

CURTIS, ADAM. (2002) *The Century of The Self. Happiness Machines.* [Online video]. Available from http://sophistryandillusion.com/videos/Adam-Curtis/The+Century+of+the+-Self+-+pt.+1+%28Happiness+Machines%29.flv.php. [Accessed on 19/11/2013]

ibid.

rise to a growing business in 'self-betterment': personal coaches, self-help or self-improvement blogs, books and magazines, all addressing the development of the psychological world of the individual faced with questions like: who am I? what is my talent? what is my passion? and what is my goal in life?

Over the past years, branding and advertising – a process of applying and visualizing ornament – emphasize the 'feeling' that a product can give you, rather than to highlight its functional abilities. This has reached the extent of, for example, a shower gel and body lotion being called *Nivea Happy* or a Starbucks slogan running: "Stay Amazed, Share the Fun". A more subtle way to underline the feeling that a brand supposedly gives you takes place through the use of melancholic images and music in advertising campaigns for example, or the visualization of personal moments of happiness through dreamy images or seemingly self-filmed moments – as if they came from our personal memory and experience.

In Fashion Journal 2009-2010, David Shah underlines this predominance of 'personal feelings' when he proposes a new social face to design, which is nowhere more visible than in the luxury market. He explains this social face as 'brand quietness' and 'modesty' which, according to him, is a reaction to 'bling' and status-ridden products. According to Henry Jenkins, director of the Comparative Media Studies Program at the Massachusetts Institute of Technology, this modesty can be observed in contemporary brands: they are expected to behave like people and offer 'products' that bring emotion through "subtle inside status marketing".✦

✦ SHAH, DAVID. (2010) Is There a New Normal? *Fashion Journal 2009-2010, Fashion Performing*

Fig. 8

postmodern society is characterized by a hedonistic neo-individualism that he calls the "second individualistic revolution", the principal features of

sphere, a loss of the meaning of the great social and political institutions, the dissolution of collective memory, the passion for new technologies,

narcissism — also denounced by Christopher Lasch in *The Culture of Narcissism*. For Lipovetsky, this individualism of the anti-authoritarian

[Online] Available from http://www.counter-currents.com/2011/06/modernity-postmodernity-hypermodernity/ [Accessed on 14/01/2015]

The next stage in the development of the intrinsic character of ornament thus takes place in a culture aimed at self-development rather than at the construction of social status and expression of character. Here we can refer to Gilles Lipovetsky's writing on modern and postmodern luxury. He states that new forms of consumption arise under the pressure of neo-individualism; forms that derive from a system or scheme of emotions and personal sensations, instead of strategies that are distinctive of a social class. These forms of consumption are not about impressing the public arena, but about the experience of personal moments – 'enjoying yourself', 'having fun' – and the sensitive emotions that are part of it. It is about the feeling that you are an extraordinary person – a motivation aimed not at decency or social appearance but at living for yourself, giving your deeper emotions priority. This means that today, the intrinsic character of ornament is determined by emotion, aimed at the 'inner self'.

When we zoom out, we can relate this contemporary intrinsic character of ornament to a shift in design mentality signaled by art critic and philosopher Boris Groys. In *The Obligation to Self-Design* he writes about the shift from design of the object to design of the human beings themselves that started with modern design. According to Groys, "it could be said that modernism substituted the design of the corpse for the design of the soul". Referring to Nietzsche's diagnosis of the death of God, he states: "In a society in which design takes over the function of religion, self-design becomes a creed." ⊘

It seems that we have made a transition from a world where we design and purchase material goods into a realm where we 'interact' with supposedly subtle, modest or social brands from which we purchase

LIPOVETSKY, GILLES. (2007) Moderne Luxe, Postmoderne Luxe.

⊘ GROYS, BORIS. (2008) The Obligation to Self – Design. *E-Flux Journal.* the-obligation-to-self-design. [Accessed on 19/06/2014]

products imbued with emotional values to buy into experiences and feelings that improve our inner selves. After the move from communicating a social identity to communicating an individual identity, design has now entered the next stage, which is aimed at the inner self. Where the American saleswoman in the documentary *The Century of Self* tells her audience that everyone has a beautiful personality and that this personality must be expressed through the way we dress, the current perspective suggests that we purchase value and meaning to design our personality or inner self instead of merely expressing it.

personality, the unconscious mind is a reservoir of feelings, thoughts, urges, and memories that are outside

According to Freud, the unconscious continues to influence our behavior and experience, even though we are

es.CHERRY, KENDRA. *Psychology. about.com* [Online] Available from http://psychology.about.com/od/

[Accessed on 30/03/2015]

Part. 5
Fashioning the Mind

The focus on emotions and improvement of the inner self in relation to consumerism and desire for the 'new' seem to come together and reach new extremes in today's experience economy. As introduced in part 2, in the early 20th century, Edward Bernays' interest in the 'inner self' led him to explore ways to anticipate the irrational aspects of the human mind, the inner feelings and the "unconscious" ᛟ, as inspired by the theories of his uncle Sigmund Freud and other developments in the field of psychology at the time. Freud's theories of hidden irrational forces in the human mind fascinated Bernays. It convinced him that it was not reason but emotion and instinct that moved the masses and made him aware that there was more involved in human decision-making than factual, rational information. He was among the first to understand that selling a product or idea by engaging consumers emotionally is more successful than appealing to their intellect. This gave him the idea to manipulate people's irrational emotions. ●

With the emergence of experience design, Bernays' ideas on the utilization of irrational behavior, inner feelings and the unconscious as tools to engage the public with a product or idea are taken to a new level. On Wikipedia the experience economy is described as follows:

> *The term Experience Economy was first described in an article published in 1998 by B. Joseph Pine II and James H. Gilmore, titled The Experience Economy. In it, they described the experience economy as the next*

● CURTIS, ADAM. (2002) *The Century of The Self. Happiness Machines.* Adam-Curtis/The+Century+of+the+-Self+-+pt.+1+%28Happiness+Ma-

economy following the agrarian economy, the industrial economy, and the most recent service economy. Pine and Gilmore argue that businesses must orchestrate memorable events for their customers, and that memory itself becomes the product – the "experience". More advanced experience businesses can begin charging for the value of the "transformation" that an experience offers, for example, as education offerings might do if they were able to participate in the value that is created by the educated individual. This, they argue, is a natural progression in the value added by the business over and above its inputs. Although the concept of the Experience Economy was born in the business field, it has crossed its frontiers to tourism, architecture, nursing, urban planners and other fields. (...) This customer behavior in society has been acknowledged by various authors. An early example is the book of Alvin Toffler, Future Shock, He talked about the upcoming "experiential industry", in which people in the "future", would be willing to allocate high percentages of their salaries to live amazing experiences. Later in 1982, Holbrook and Hirschman's pioneering article "The Experiential Aspects of Consumption: Consumer Fantasies, Feelings, and Fun" in the Journal of Consumer Research (Vol. 9, #2), discussed emotional experiences linked to products and services.

[Online]. Available from: http://en.wikipedia.org/wiki/The_Experience_Economy. [Accessed: 20/3/2014]

Both experience design and the approach of Bernays, can be described as methods that aim to engage the consumer on an emotional level. The difference lies in the goals that are supposed to be achieved through this engagement. In the article *From the object to the invisible: Retail experience within space, fashion and body* Luca Marchetti, writing about experience design, discusses a relational model on experience and personal involvement that he refers to as 'psychology of the optimal experience' or 'flow'. "According to this theory, optimal experience is perceived as a flux, in the sense that it carries us forward, leaving behind those elements of awareness that have the potential to distract us from the current situation. (…) The aim is not to reach a goal but to remain within the optimal flux."*

In experience design, addressing consumers on an emotional, psychological level and making sure they leave behind those elements of awareness that have the potential to distract them, come about through interaction. This is often obvious with brands that stimulate active participation of the user or consumer, sometimes through digital applications but also through retail environments that stimulate an interactive experience. For example, the Nike store in the fashion island lifestyle center in Newport Beach, California, features an in-store workout studio for group or personal training sessions•. It is important though that the goal of offering this training is not only to sell a new pair of shoes or a new shirt or to engage the consumer with a material product. In these training sessions, interaction or, as B. Joseph Pine II & James H. Gilmore would say: the "transformation" as an ongoing activity, can be the 'product' or goal itself. Although related to the unconscious and irrational motives that Bernays

* MARCHETTI, LUCA. (2009) From the Object to the Invisible: Retail … Press, d'JongeHond, p. 177.

• NIKE (2014) *Nike women's-only store with fitness studio opens in Newport* … newport-beach-california-combines-best-of-women-s-products- …

used as a starting point, the difference with Bernays' approach is that the goal of experience design is transformation, not engagement with a material product per se.

The term 'experience economy' stems from staging experiences to bring about such transformations. According to B. Joseph Pine II and James H. Gilmore, the key elements to these experiences are "fantasies, feelings and fun". An example of this focus on fantasies, feelings and fun is *Burberry Kiss*, a collaboration with Google that allows users to kiss their touch screens and send their lip prints to loved ones. Another example is Nivea Happy, which functionally does not differ from any other lotion, but does promise something else: happiness. Within experience design it is exactly these emotional elements that are used as constructed added value; a symbolic value-ornament. Bringing together emotion as a means and as a goal illustrates that, today, feeling is used to sell feeling; sometimes clearly spelled out on the 'product' to be sold and sometimes almost without interference by the existence of a relevant 'material product'.

"A central feature of the paradigm shift from traditional applied art to modern design [in the early 20th century, *FdV*] was just this extension of the will to design from the world of things to that of human beings themselves – understood as one thing among many."

Referring to a contemporary desire to design the inner self, emotion could be one of the things we need. And it is clear that within experience design, despite different approaches - some more direct than others - emotion is not only viewed upon as a means but also as an end. While Bernays used emotion to sell a 'product', in experience design we can

omer Experience. [Online] 27th March 2014. Available from http://www.

rys-blurred-lines-the-integrated-customer-experience/[Accessed in January 2015]

[Online] 1 (12/2008). Available from: http://www.e-flux.com/journal/

Ibid. × question if the experience of an emotion or a state of mind can be the actual commodity or service. In Groys' *Obligation to Self-Design* we can recognize the pressure that comes with designing ourselves, which leads to questions about ways and techniques to make this self-design possible. × In the specific development of 'self-design', experience economy and the associated experience design seem to play an essential role. Perhaps, by proposing a fixed range of emotions – or rather value-ornaments with intrinsic characters of emotions – staged in experiences to transform the inner self with, the experience economy anticipates, or even partly creates, the question of how to design the self. What then, could be the effect on the user if experience design would fashion or offer a certain 'state of mind'?

Fig. 9

Metamorfose, een Hermès story

HERMÈS

PARIS

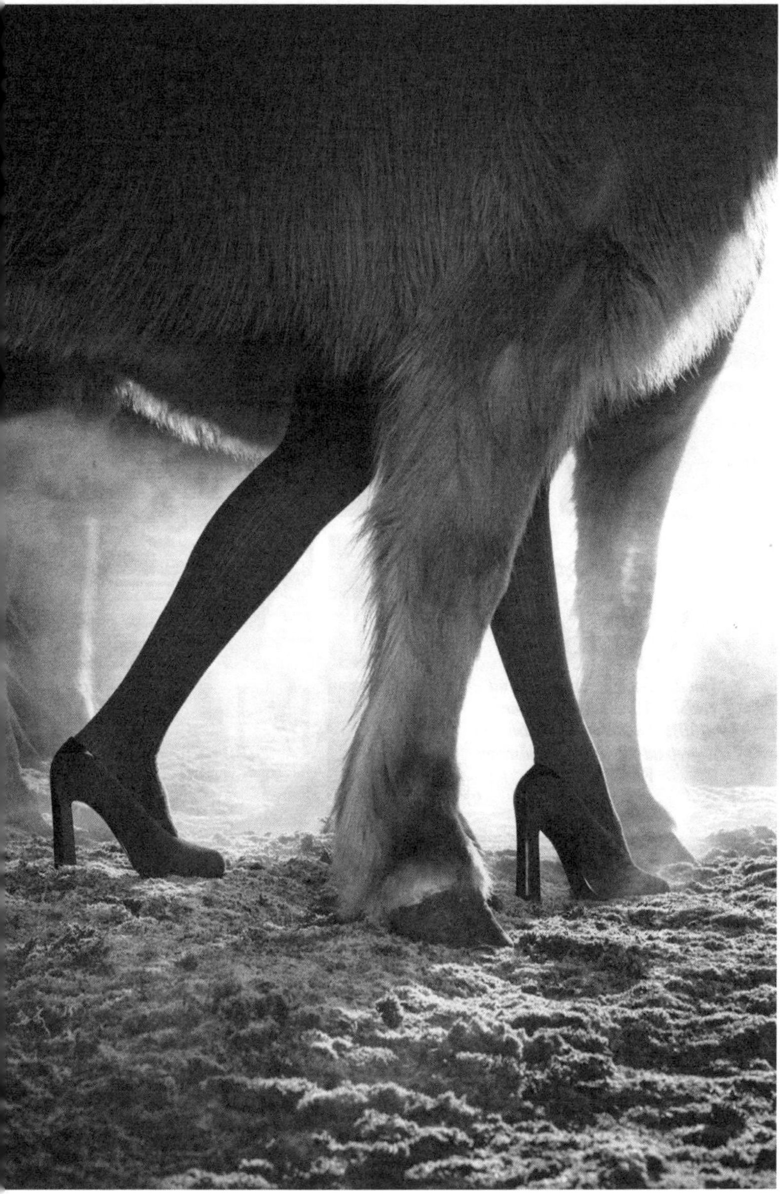

Part 6.
Today's Ornament, a Fleeting State of Mind

From ornament as tangible decoration on the surface to constructed symbolism and value linked to products used as a form of expression, we have now arrived at the ornament as a constructed value that is developed with the aim to engage and configure the inner self of the consumer. We find these added values mainly in the form of brands and designer identities and their stories constructed from emotions that can only be grasped through an experience and the consequent memory of this experience. Building the 'inner self', instead of just expressing it, has repudiated the material product and made this new immaterial ornament the most essential ornament in contemporary consumer society. It has become the starting point in the design process, taking over the position of the material object, to an extent that makes it impossible to ask if ornament can be omitted in the way Loos requested from the cobbler. More importantly, this ornament has become a stand-alone characteristic that has gained power over the practical and material value of a so-called commodity, and can even exist on its own, without the commodity - in fact it can become the commodity. This is how 'today's ornament' is to be understood.

Fig. 10

FUN
FUN FUN
PULLOVER

Today's ornament and the literal 'traditional' ornament are both tools to change 'style', they both stimulate obsolescence; cost more labor time in comparison to a 'smooth' or unadorned object; and imply a certain aesthetic, or in Loos's words: they impose taste. However, as has been outlined in previous parts there are differences. In short: contrary to the literal ornament, today's ornament can be seen as a stand-alone, intangible element that has no relationship with the 'materiality' of a product and only becomes visible through 'mediators' like magazines, advertising, shopping spaces, products, etcetera. In addition, contrary to Loos's critique on the literal ornament, the increased labor time needed to produce today's ornament is paid for by the consumer.♦ Also, while both the literal and today's ornament have a strong connection with effectuating feelings, they differ in how they do this. In the realm of the literal ornament we could approach ornament as a material, tangible or visible mediator that is directly placed upon the object or wearer, which may evoke a certain feeling or value related to the object or person it is placed upon. Within the realm of today's ornament these feelings and values that are clearly supposed to be evoked, are described in a pre-conceived plan and are often literally spelled out in the various 'advertising techniques' used to address the owner's mind. Revisiting the Starbucks slogan "Stay Amazed, Share the Fun" and the Nivea Happy body lotion, the effect that the literal ornament could possibly achieve – fun, amazement and happiness in these examples – is within today's ornament very consciously used as the starting point and spelled out for the consumer.

♦ TED. (2004) *What Consumers Want.* [Online video]. February 2004. Available from http://www.ted.com/talks/joseph_pine_on_what_consumers_want.html. [Accessed on 04/04/2014]. In this Ted Talk Joseph Pine talks about how a cup of coffee at Starbucks is more expensive than a cup of coffee at a regular coffee shop. This higher price at Starbucks can in fact be directly related to the constructed value of the Starbucks ambiance and its experience.

The various forms of ornament – tangible, intangible, to express or to develop the inner self, with a 'subtle' message or clearly spelled out – make sure it is present in almost all arenas of daily life. In *Design and Crime (And Other Diatribes)* Hal Foster describes a strong echo of Art Nouveau in the present: "(…) that we live in another era of blurred disciplines, of objects treated as mini-subjects."[✈] It is an era of Total Design, of *Gesamtkunstwerk*. Together with the literal or 'traditional' ornament, today's ornament creates the possibility for the contemporary designer to ornament on different levels and to transfer this ornament from one object to the other, making it possible to present the consumer with a wide array of choices to 'dress' oneself: the outer self with clothing, accessories, interior, technology, transport, etcetera, and the inner self with feelings, value and experience. In combination this could be defined as the ultimate Total Design. Ornament that occupies multiple areas of life links to the term 'lifestyle', often used in contemporary consumer society, suggesting that life in all its layers can, to some extent, be styled or designed.

Today's ornament can be seen as a superlative and essential part of this total design. By adding emotion, experience and fantasy to the list of things that can be designed, today's ornament does not just seem to aim at the design of life but at the design of human beings themselves.[°] Where the literal ornament designs or dresses the human body or expresses its status, today's ornament of emotions dresses the inner self. Today's ornament, clearly grounded in a general desire and obligation to develop our inner selves and in today's experience economy, could therefore be defined as a way to design or achieve a certain intrinsic modus, a 'state of mind' or 'fashion'.

✈ FOSTER, HAL. (2002) *Design and Crime, And Other Diatribes* London/ New York: Verso. p. 14.

° GROYS, BORIS. (2008) The Obligation to Self – Design. *E-Flux Journal.* [Online] 1 (12/2008). Available from http://www.e-flux.com/journalthe-obligation-to-self-design. [Accessed on 19/06/2014]

The reception room was almost frighteningly free of decoration. There was a low table made from a single thick plank. Nothing lay on it – no ashtray, no tablecloth. No pictures adorned the walls. No clocks, no calendars, no vases. No sideboard, no magazines, no books. The floor had an antique rug so faded that its pattern could not be discerned, (...)

In *White Walls, Designer Dresses*, Mark Wigley points out that Loos does not criticize ornament because it so easily succumbs to fashion. Rather, ornament is, by definition, fashion itself.[☠] Approached from the realm of the literal ornament, as a so-called 'superficial' addition, this statement could be interpreted to mean that fashion is a surface layer, a 'sauce'. However, considering the equation of ornament and fashion from the realm of today's ornament leads to a completely different possible definition of fashion: if today's ornament can be defined as a state of mind, and ornament is to be defined as fashion, would it be feasible to conclude that contemporary fashion is a state of mind?

In comparison with today's ornament, fashion too could be defined as an intangible affair that only becomes obtainable, visible and useable through 'expressions' like shopping spaces, 'dressing up', writings, advertising, events, magazines, etcetera. However, more importantly: if fashion, like today's ornament, is a state of mind then it has a pronounced specification: fleetingness. This fleetingness has always been acknowledged as an important characteristic of fashion but it becomes even more enhanced when applied within the realm of today's ornament. With respect to today's ornament, mainly built of intangible experiences and feelings, we have to consider that emotion or a state of mind itself is normally a fleeting experience clearly related to psychological obsolescence. Adding to this, there is a strong possibility that buying into an emotion or experience that is artificially staged by a designer who imposes his or her taste or aesthetic increases this fleetingness and subsequently stimulates a craving for a new feeling, a new state of mind.

London: MIT Press. p. 174.

In the experience economy, the ephemerality of feeling and the desire to improve our emotional world are at the core of today's ornament, which functions as a tool of psychological obsolescence. This extra dimension in total design accelerates the temporality of commodities and strengthens the ornament's relation to fashion. Today's ornament consists of fantasies and feelings that directly address the psyche rather than the physicality of the body: the desire to develop the inner self and attain a certain state of mind. In short: today's ornament is a contemporary form of fashion. And as it is not just a state of mind, but a fleeting state of mind, changing every season, perhaps it could best be defined as the ultimate form of fashion?

Part 7.
Clothes as Souvenirs

Throughout design history, ornament has primarily been presented as an element that is opposed to the 'core' of something and understood as a dressing to enrich the 'real' object or the 'naked' body. However, this dressing, or ornament, can also be understood as an additional layer, a façade that conceals. In fashion, concealment is often seen as a generator of desires and fantasies of what lies 'underneath'. When searching for the 'real' object underneath, the question is how to undress it - and what will be revealed.

Loos wanted to reveal the value of certain materials, craftsmanship, and individual honesty.✪ Today we can recognize a similar development in the longing for pure materials and honest production. This longing has been deployed by brands in advertisements on packaging, in magazines and in commercials that give an insight into the production process. Strategies may include mentioning where the product is made, tracing the steps of the production processes and sometimes even portraying the individual laborer who made it. In this way the production and material character of the object seems to be revealed and displayed. The logical assumption would be that this can be defined as de-ornamentation clearing the product it of all its clutter. In this case however, displaying signs of production and material characteristics is just an elaboration of a symbolic ornament that can be clustered with the much used term authenticity. Authenticity is clearly deployed as a commercial value-ornament because the provided insight into the production process is nearly always staged and

✪ GROYS, BORIS. (2008) The Obligation to Self – Design. *E-Flux Journal.* [Online] 1 (12/2008). Available from the-obligation-to-self-design. [Accessed on 19/06/2014]

Fig. 12

© American Colony, Jerusale

ROMANIZED ARAB ARTISANS CARVED THESE DELICATE DESIGNS

The modern Bedouin has no religious scruples or superstitious fear of the capitals of El Khazna, a he had of the figures above them; therefore they have escaped unmolested (see page 151).

ROMANIZED ARAB ARTISAN CARVED THESE DELICATE DESIGNS

only meant to create the illusion of craftsmanship and 'realness' – consequently raising the price of the product. In this case the impression of an object's production process is used to create symbolic value. As a result, the real object is concealed by a false representation of a process that suggests it shows the real object. But what are the implications for the material object when the representation is seen as 'the real object'?

Even though in contemporary design and fashion – where the emphasis lies on intangible values – the object appears to be the most materially fixed element, it has become part of the decor itself: the material object now functions as a prop. This idea refers to B. Joseph Pine II and James H. Gilmore who argue that goods can be considered as props for the directing of experiences set within a theatre.◆ Just as (symbolic) ornaments have become commodities, objects and products have become props, especially in the experience economy, which is mainly staged within a so-called theatre, described as the on and off stage work of business.⌘ Props are objects that have no actual function beyond being used to dress up a theatre stage, movie set or photograph. Functioning as a carrier of meaning, or value, the object does not even have to function properly; it only has to look good or convincing as part of the staged experience. In this case, following the 'traditional' views on ornament as an addition, it is possible to draw the conclusion that the material product has now become the ornament as addressed in part 3.

The experience economy makes today's ornament visible and obtainable through shopping spaces, advertisements, celebrities, shows, videos, personnel, and through the products themselves. In fashion,

◆ PINE II, JOSEPH B. & GILMORE, JAMES H. (2011) *The Experience Economy*. Updated Edition. Boston:

⌘ Ibid.

a diverse range of media such as advertisements, blogs, magazines, celebrities, shopping spaces, perfume, fashion shows and accessories has been used to present symbolic value for many decades. But today even the clothes themselves can be added to this range of media, because they have lost their function as the starting point in the design process to the stories and ideas they now serve to illustrate. So to what extent has the character and quality of clothing adapted to its new place in the design process and its definition as a prop?

To a large extent, fashion today takes place on blogs. This is a two-dimensional context, mainly focusing on still images rather than on moving images, and is aimed at viewing a piece of clothing, not wearing it. Consequently, the object seems to completely lose its relationship to a three-dimensional, moving body and with that, it loses its functional, material character. It is disconnected from its original realm of use. This has led some designers to start designing with the idea of Internet and its flat, square images in mind, as discussed in the conversation *For Fashion's Sake.*• Essentially, these designers consider the way a piece of clothing will look best on the Internet as the most important attribute and they completely ignore the aspect of practical use on a moving body. Of course, the same can be said of traditional magazines and fashion photography – and this underlines an approach to fashion that has little connection to clothing as objects of use and can therefore function as an abstract affair. It clearly illustrates the difference between fashion and clothing.

The decline of the material quality of products that is interlinked with mass produced confection, has now also entered the luxury industry and can be easily and directly related to the idea of commodities as props.

FA$HION'S S@KE. In conversation. [Online video]. 2014. Available from http://showstudio.com/project/ [Accessed on 25/07/ 2014]. Frances Corner, Michel Gaubert, Stephen Jones, Lutz Huelle and Ryan Aguilar- Seminar 2014 chaired by Dan Thawley and Lou Stoppard.

In *How Luxury Lost its Lustre* (2007) Dana Thomas writes about a strong concentration on elements that can be defined as part of today's ornament in the fashion world: shopping palaces, star celebrities, actresses, stylists, perfumes, bags and interior design. She demonstrates how this focus forced luxury brands to cut costs using cheaper materials, which is clearly affecting the material quality of the product. For example, she compares a pair of Prada trousers bought in 2002, to a Prada cocktail dress from 1992.

THOMAS, DANA. (2007) *Deluxe, How Luxury Lost its Lustre*. New York: Penguin Press

> *I put them on, and the gentle passing of my foot ripped the hem out. I put my hand in the pocket, and it tore away from its seam. (...) I hadn't had those pants on ten minutes and they were literally falling apart at the seams. I mentioned this to a former Prada design assistant. "It's the thread," he told me. "It's cheaper and breaks easily." When I told him about my gorgeous dress from 1992 that was solid as a Rolls, he nodded. "That was then," he said with a sigh.*

While the general decline of the material and functional character of products is a reality, the opposing focus on craftsmanship and so-called authenticity in contemporary design has actually put various products on the market that are materially more valuable. But when we consider the context of today's ornament: does the purchase of better-made products really prevent us from discarding them sooner than necessary or do we still replace them because the feeling that they represent has become obsolete? If the latter is the case, we must question if the investment in material and functional quality really has the potential to add to the lifespan of a product.

Fig. 13

BEWITCHED, BOTHERED, BEWILDERED

Long talks, chilly sunsets (or is that a sunrise?), and an inspired meeting of the minds are all hallmarks of a memorable holiday—or an ethereal love affair. Miu Miu dress ($2,815); select Miu Miu boutiques. Céline sneakers. Details, see In This Issue.

Even if we approach the purchase of experiences and feelings as a positive thing, we will still be confronted with the fact that it has become harder to differentiate the functional object of use from the object as prop. In *Le Mot Dans La Mode* Ulrich Lehmann writes about a development in texts in fashion magazines in and around the 19th century, where fashion is described as "spherical images", mentioning the name or sphere of a dress design without describing its 'material' characteristics. "To evoke the dress without description generated a self-referential discourse that assumed knowledge on behalf of the readership in regard to cut, fabric, colour, etc. of dressing, so that its actual materiality was largely superfluous."° The approach of describing objects as spherical images or, in other words, as a feeling, is embodied in today's ornament and applied to a range of products: cars, furniture, kitchenware, body care products, electronics, etcetera. Meanwhile, the larger part of the users know very little about the raw materials, functional qualities and processes of the products they purchase. Telling prop from functional object becomes even more difficult when technical or material quality becomes a common brand-value and an element of ornament instead of a materialistic and technical characteristic.× This brings about a question of 'realness' and the definition of ornament as a concealer, masquerading the inner 'true' object. When we picture a situation in which we are aware of the fact that objects mainly act as carriers of value and feelings and we buy them with this in mind, then poor functional quality should not per definition be a problem. However, the all-encompassing impact of branding and experience design does bring up the question: where are the things that are really meant for practical use to come from? What

° LEHMANN, ULRICH. (2009) Le mot dans la mode. In: Brand, Jan, Teunis-

× It also questions the focus and motivation on the use of innovative

provement for the functioning of the product or is technological renewal

is apparent is that clothing has been swallowed by fashion, as is the case for many other product groups.

With the consumer longing to develop their inner self and the designer offering stories and identities constructed from 'feelings, fantasies and fun', the object of clothing is mainly purchased to grasp the experience and the consumer wears it hoping to develop the inner self through reviving memories each time they dress. Could this constitute the definition of use within today's experience economy? Especially in the experience economy, with the presence of today's ornament, the lifespan of products has been reduced, as all that is required from the garment at this point is that it is a visual representation or carrier of a feeling, of an experience – and little more. If these commodities are mainly produced to represent a feeling, a fantasy or a memory, has the commodity become merely a souvenir?

On this notion of the object as souvenir Pine and Gilmore state: "Selling memorabilia associated with an experience provides one approach to extending, an experience (...)."[▣] With this understanding, can the palpable props of fashion, like clothing, be defined as souvenirs? Souvenirs that do what fashion is about: to capture a fleeting, intangible experience, a state of mind, 'wearing' a different feeling with each change of clothes? Has the fashion object reached its perfect form as a souvenir?

Economy. Updated Edition. Boston: Harvard Business Review Press. p. 86.

Fig. 14

" yeah, but man,
that was good."
" How good?"
"Like there's no past
or future anymore."
" The pure present is
an ungraspable advance
of the past devouring
the future. In truth,
all sensation is already
memory."

Part 8.
The User as Ornamentor

In *Design and Crime* Hal Foster elaborates on an allegorical skit about "a poor little rich man" written by Adolf Loos before he wrote *Ornament and Crime.* In this piece Loos claims that the suffocating nature of an Art Nouveau room "taxed the owner's brain" because it lacked any space for "future living and striving, developing and desiring".○ In 1912, Viennese journalist Karl Kraus referred to this as a lack of "running room" or "Spielraum". The premise behind this running room comes from the notice of allowing an idea, place, material or object enough room to change. The risk is that this 'room to wiggle' diminishes even more when we look at today's ornament in relation to personal emotional space. According to Loos, from the perspective of the literal 'traditional' ornament, the space for the user's own value begins to diminish from the moment the consumer stops going to a cobbler to get a pair of new shoes, and instead has to choose from a mass-produced selection. Boris Groys wrote similarly in *The Obligation to Self-Design* (2008): "However, consumers become prisoners of total design to a much larger degree than ever before, inasmuch they can no longer delegate their aesthetic decisions to others."* This again connects to Loos's view on ornamentation as a form of imposing taste. How does this work with today's ornament as a value- and feeling-based ornament? If the above mentioned notion – that space for personal values is reduced – is applied to the realm of today's ornament it outlines a scenario in which emotions or 'states of mind' are to be chosen from a mass-produced selection designed and predetermined by a designer. Considering the designer from the perspective of

○ FOSTER, HAL. (2002) *Design and Crime, And Other Diatribes* London/ New York: Verso. p. 15

* GROYS, BORIS. (2008) The Obligation to Self – Design. *E-Flux Journal* [Online] 1 (12/2008). Available from the-obligation-to-self-design. [Accessed on 19/06/2014]

design history and design discourse, as the creator of ornament – and thus the creator of a subjectively 'added' value – she or he seems to have an extremely powerful position. Adolf Loos presents a similar claim when comparing the act of ornamentation to imposing taste and aesthetic. Likewise Roland Barthes writes: "A tree is a tree. Yes, of course. But a tree as expressed by Minou Drouet is no longer quite a tree, it is a tree which is decorated, adapted to a certain kind of consumption, laden with literary self-indulgence, revolt, images, in short with a type of social usage which is added to pure matter."▾ The powerful position of the designer raises the issue of who, actually, should be entitled to develop this contemporary ornament, emotional value or state of mind. Who defines the feeling that comes with an object or situation? Trained as a professional (fashion) designer I am trained to ornament, to construct this 'fashion' or state of mind. I learned to develop ornament subjectively, from my own tastes and preferences. How should the contemporary designer deal with this position?

In addition to my role as an ornamentor I am also a user. The user versus maker, reader versus writer and the shifting of these roles, is often referred to in contemporary culture. Highlighting the dynamics between these two roles can be useful when redefining the role of the maker and user in the realm of today's ornament. In *The Practice of Everyday Life*● (1984) De Certeau examines the ways in which people individualize mass culture, altering things, from utilitarian objects to street plans to rituals, laws and language, in order to make them their own. De Certeau discusses tactics versus strategies – strategies being the structures and systems imposed by, for example, politics. De Certeau states that the ap-

Today'. In: HARRISON, CHARLES AND WOOD, PAUL. (eds.) (2011) *Art in Theory 1900 – 2000 An Anthology* New Jersey: Blackwell Publishing. p. 694.

Practice of Everyday Life. Berkeley: University of California Press.

propriation of these strategies does not exist in passive consumption but in the use itself and the tactics that are developed by the user during the use phase. Roland Barthes in *The Death of the Author* (1967)[♃] also writes about the roles of the writer and reader, which are comparable to the roles of the maker and user and to the idea of strategies and tactics. Barthes states that the essential meaning of a work depends on the impressions of the reader, rather than the passions or tastes of the writer; "a text's unity lies not in its origins," or its creator, "but in its destination," or its audience.

Considering De Certeau's and Barthes' views allows the understanding that the tactics with which the user applies and rewrites the narrative codes can be a means to add personal value to the 'object' or 'product' and in this way surpass the strategy that is imposed by an 'author', a designer, brand or ornamentor. The act of adding personal value could be observed through customization and appropriation of infrastructure and modes of use. An example in fashion of users empowered to surpass strategies would be Russian home dressmakers bypassing governmentally imposed dress rules during Socialism by circulating and adjusting paper patterns of Western fashionable dresses.[⊙] In the experience economy and the accompanying branding strategies, the act of value production is already approached as an interplay or co-creation between user and maker, inviting the user to apply their tactics to enhance the 'value-in-use'. But because this co-creation takes place in defined commercial settings with a commercial goal and today's value-ornament is characterized by feelings, the actual input of the consumer as co-creator is debatable.

♃ BARTHES, ROLAND. (1976) *The Death of the Author.* [Online] Available from http://www.ubuweb.com/

⊙ BARTLETT, DJURDJA. (2010) *Fashion East, The Spectre that Haunted Socialism.* Cambridge / London: The

From the perspective of De Certeau and Barthes, today's ornament can be defined as a strategy, a "narrative code".* We are familiar with feelings used as a strategy to enhance the purchase of 'products', but it has become clear that within the realm of today's ornament emotions, or a state of mind, are not approached as a tool but as the essence, as the goal. Today's ornament can thus be considered a narrative code (linking to designers as storytellers) that carries certain values or emotions, sometimes addressing them to 'objects' and 'situations' but also existing as a stand-alone 'state of mind' (using objects as props). In this case the characteristics of today's ornament lead to a contradiction within the roles of the maker and the user in relation to tactics and strategies.

> *"The experiences we have affect who we are, what we can accomplish, and where we are going, and we increasingly ask companies to stage experiences that change us. Human beings have always sought out new and exciting experiences to learn and grow, develop and improve, mend and reform. But as the world progresses further into the Experience Economy, much that was previously obtained through noneconomic activity will increasingly be found in the domain of commerce. That represents a significant change. It means that to obtain what we once sought for free, we now pay a fee."*◆

ble from http://www.ubuweb.com/papers/. [Accessed on 10/10/2014], p. 2.

Economy. Updated Edition. Boston: Harvard Business Review Press. p. 241-242.

Fig. 15

This rug was "grown" in Minnesota.

If, in the future, subjective elements like emotions, which are inherently connected to the personal space of human beings, are to be paid for, the power relation between the maker and the user becomes quite controversial. However, by mentioning that fantasies, feelings and experiences – previously 'non-economic activities' – will not remain free in the future, B. Joseph Pine II and James H. Gilmore indirectly allude to the fact that presently, these are elements that we are capable of creating ourselves. In fact, they illustrate that the emotional ornament can be seen as an act of ornamenting that could actually be achieved from scratch by the user, without a commercial entity setting the terms, and therefore potentially places the user in the position of ornamentor. While seemingly straightforward, this statement, from a design perspective, brings to light a different approach to the 'act of ornamenting' and the various roles within this act.

If designing can, according to Charles Saumarez Smith, be defined as putting together the processes of 'building', decorating and ornamenting in a preconceived plan*, the difference between the designer and the user would be that the user does not develop ornament – and thus feeling and value – in a *pre-conceived* plan. For example, when we would, somehow (in an almost unimaginable situation) acquire an unmarked piece of clothing in an unmarked situation the emotional added value, or ornament, would only arrive with the acts of wearing, using, washing, and repairing the piece. Value would be produced through interacting with a body, mind and context. All of this would be derived and 'grown' from use instead of constructed in a pre-conceived plan. Could it be that authentic emotional ornament in relation to the user arrives with use?

and Domestic Interior in Eighteenth-Century England. London: Pimlico.

Fig. 16

The fifth property of cloth is that it has “living” qualities. Cloth absorbs. It takes in physical substances – bodily fluids such as saliva, sweat, and blood, and gaseous substances from the air, such as odor and smoke. It absorbs sound. Universally, it is also felt to take in and absorb more invisible energies. We are all familiar with the idea that someone’s clothing comes to hold their essence; clothes are often spoken of, in fact, as a kind of “second skin” that seems to hold the living substance of the wearer. (…)

He was there in the wrinkles of the elbows…he was there in the stains at the bottom… he was there in the smell.

When considering a 'pre-ornamented' piece of clothing, this same process of use could possibly rewrite the narrative code, but always with traces of the pre-fabricated, constructed value-ornament remaining. To the user, the act of defining our own emotional value-ornament to a product is a process of washing, folding, using, wearing and interacting. It is not a very anarchistic act and does not have to be, but this mode of thinking can expose the mechanisms of today's ornament and, in doing so, open up the opportunity to recognize the value of developing ornament from a user's perspective, i.e. rewriting it to our personal insight. It leads to a curiosity about the types of rewrites and codes that could emerge, either spontaneous or well-considered.

When we bypass the designer, who combines building and ornamenting in a pre-conceived plan, and shift to the ornamentor who focuses only on ornament – the role in which most so-called designers function today – it is possible to imagine that everyone can be an ornamentor. The striking difference however, between so-called designers and users lies first of all in the order of the process. Does 'dressing' or constructing ornament occur before or after 'building'? Is the dressing or emotional ornament constructed in a pre-conceived 'building plan' or does it arrive with use? These questions indirectly also emphasize the difference between a professional and an amateur, a commercial goal and a non-commercial goal – which in turn raises new questions. In the case of today's ornament, the amateur seems to create the most authentic and exclusive ornament and as such transcends or subverts the professional ornamentor. When approaching experience design and its output as a system, a strategy or a code – that can be defined as the ultimate form of design, where feelings become ‘designable’ – it carries an inherent flaw from a commercial perspective: it offers something a user can develop him or herself in a stronger, more authentic way without the need for technical knowledge, material, machinery or great financial resources. However, the vulnerability of this system can only be exploited when the act of dressing or ornamenting is unveiled and users become aware of their power. This is not customization or appropriation, but creation. Could this herald the end of contemporary (fashion) design and its designer?

Part 9.
To conclude, for now

It is clear that value in relation to fashion today is not something that is added but something that is at the very core: it is the starting point in the process of production and consumption, which means that the material object and the symbolic value change position. Ornament is no longer to be seen as merely a layer or decoration to add. “Decoration is no longer applied to an object; it is the object”.* Thus it is ornament that today’s designers or ornamentors, focus on. This shift in position changes the characteristics of the ‘products’ we produce and consume, the roles of the makers and users and the accompanying processes of development and use.

* FRAME. (2014) Frame Product and Form, in the Mix. *Frame*. 99. (Jul/Aug 2014), p. 145. A quote from Faro

Although ‘old ornaments’ continue to exist next to ‘new ornaments’, the contemporary value-ornament, which is mostly expressed in brand strategies, identities and storytelling, is put forward with great determination. In today’s experience economy centered on designing emotional experiences, this dominant value-ornament is characterized by ‘feelings, fantasies and fun’, creating transformations and a particular state of mind. Just like the so-called literal ornament this ‘feeling-ornament’ is created by a designer or ornamentor who not only decides on the look but also on the feeling ‘products’ should inspire.

The emphasis on feeling shows a direct relation to psychological obsolescence aiming at the ‘owner’s mind’ as discussed by Vance Packard•, which has today taken the shape of selling feelings almost or entirely without interference of a relevant material object. Thus ‘products’ are turned into props and

• PACKARD, VANCE. (1960) *The Waste Makers*. United States: Vance Packard Inc. (first edition)

emotion into the essence. The fleeting character of a feeling, in general, enhances the temporary nature of this kind of ornament and the material objects and contexts it is attached to. Easily functioning in the fast cycle of fashion, in this case it focuses on the inner self rather than the outer appearance of the user. In short, designers currently focus on creating a 'fleeting state of mind'. This focus strengthens the position of Loos[♦] and Foster[✚] on the effect ornament supposedly has on the user and shows that this ornament evolves even more towards the design of 'the self' as Boris Groys[❦] describes it. This design of the self also relates to Lipovetsky's neo-individualism to which the experience, enjoyment and emotions are central.[✳] The experience economy and its designers or ornamentors elaborate on this by offering a fixed range of fantasies and feelings to choose from. It is possibly this focus on the inner self adds another dimension to Simmel's tension between the social identity and individual identity that defines fashion.[♠]

What B. Joseph Pine II and James H. Gilmore, the authors of *The Experience Economy*[♣] inadvertently reveal through their arguments is that fantasies, feelings and experiences (a state of mind) are free and that we can produce them ourselves from scratch, independent from any commercial suggestions or brand-initiated co-creation. With this in mind: if it were possible to transfer the entire act of value production in relation to 'products and services' from the professional designer to the user, how would this affect future perspectives of the user and maker, and what kind of system would it enable for fashion cycles and products?

♦
LOOS, ADOLF. (1908) *Ornament and Crime.* [Online]. Available from http://www2.gwu.edu/~art/Temporary_SL/177/pdfs/Loos.pdf. [Accessed on 10/10/2007]

✚
FOSTER, HAL. (2002) *Design and Crime, And Other Diatribes* London/New York: Verso.

❦
GROYS, BORIS. (2008) The Obligation to Self – Design. *E-Flux Journal.* [Online] 1 (12/2008). Available from http://www.e-flux.com/journal/the-obligation-to-self-design. [Accessed on 19/06/2014]

✳
LIPOVETSKY, GILLES. (2007) Moderne Luxe, Postmoderne Luxe. In: Brand, Jan, Teunissen, José. *Mode & Accessoires.* Uitgeverij Terra Lannoo bv.

♠
SIMMEL, GEORG (1904) *Fashion.* [Online] (09/2010). Available from http://sites.middlebury.edu/individualandthesociety/files/2010/09/Simmel.fashion.pdf [Accessed on 15/01/2015]

♣
PINE II, JOSEPH B. & GILMORE, JAMES H. (2011) *The Experience Economy.* Updated Edition. Boston: Harvard Business Review Press.

Femke de Vries works as an artist/researcher in the field of fashion where she explores the interaction between clothing as (material) objects of use and fashion as a process of value production.

She aims to expose the workings of fashion through deconstruction and re-readings from various perspectives. Seeking alternative scenarios for makers and users she considers the role of fashion communication formats, cultural/social/economical references and material culture, questioning hierarchies and emphasising the physical reality of use. Her research led practice is driven by collaboration and results in works that combine visual cultures, approaches to textile and clothing, theory and educational programs.

She has a background in Fashion Design (Amsterdam Fashion Institute) and Fashion Strategy (ArtEZ Fashion Masters). Projects/works have taken shape through collaborations with and presentations at: Alicia Framis, Droog Design, e-flux/TimeBank, Galerie BlockC, Harvard Design Magazine, Hordaland Kunstsenter, Joke Robaard, MetropolisM, Np3 and Stroom Den Haag.

In collaboration with Onomatopee she published two books: Fashioning Value – Undressing Ornament and Dictionary Dressings (2016). Through positions at various universities including ArtEZ Fashion Masters, WDKA (Willem de Kooning Academy), HKU (University of the Arts Utrecht) and KABK (Royal Academy of Art The Hague) she developed specialized educational programs and tutored graduation research projects.

ARENDT, HANNAH. (1998) *The Human Condition* [Online] Available from http://sduk.us/afterwork/arendt_the_human_condition.pdf [Accessed on 9/01/2015]

BARTHES, ROLAND. (1956) 'Myth Today'. In: HARRISON, CHARLES AND WOOD, PAUL. (eds.) (2011) *Art in Theory 1900 – 2000 An Anthology of Changing Ideas.* Hoboken New Jersey: Blackwell Publishing.

BARTHES, ROLAND. (1976) *The Death of the Author.* [Online] Available from http://www.ubuweb.com/papers/. [Accessed on 10/10/2014]

BARTLETT, DJURDJA. (2010) *Fashion East, The Spectre that Haunted Socialism.* Cambridge / London: The MIT Press.

BLANCHARD, TAMSIN. (2013) Fashion & Graphic Design. In Teunissen, José with Voet, Hanka van der with Brand, Jan. (eds.) *Couture Graphique.* Houten: Uitgeverij Terra Lannoo bv.

CERTEAU, MICHEL DE. (1984) *The Practice of Everyday Life.* Berkeley: University of California Press.

CHERRY, KENDRA. *Psychology.about.com* [Online] Available from http://psychology.about.com/od/uindex/g/def_unconscious.htm [Accessed on 30/03/2015]

CHUKHROV, KETI. (2011) Towards the Space of the General: On Labor Beyond Materiality and Immateriality. In: *e-flux journal. Are You Working Too Much? Post Fordism, Precarity, and the Labor of Art.* Sternberg Press.

CURTIS, ADAM. (2002) *The Century of The Self. Happiness Machines.* [Online video]. Available from http://sophistryandillusion.com/videos/Adam-Curtis/The+Century+of+the+-Self+-+pt.+1+%28Happiness+Machines%29.flv.php. [Accessed on 19/11/2013]

DAVIS, SCOTT. (2014) *Burberry's Blurred Lines: The Integrated Customer Experience.* [Online] 27th March 2014. Available from http://www.forbes.com/sites/scottdavis/2014/03/27/burberrys-blurred-lines-the-integrated-customer-experience/ [Accessed in January 2015]

FOSTER, HAL. (2002) *Design and Crime, And Other Diatribes* London/New York: Verso.

FRAME. (2014) Frame Product and Form, in the Mix. *Frame.* 99. (Jul/Aug 2014).

FRANK, JULIA. (2013) *Tom Ford's 14 Tips on Building a Fashion Brand.* [Online] 14/11/2013. Available from *Vogue.com* http://www.vogue.com.au/fashion/news/tom+fords+14+tips+on+building+a+fashion+brand, 28189. [Accessed in May 2014]

GROYS, BORIS. (2008) The Obligation to Self – Design. *E-Flux Journal.* [Online] 1 (12/2008). Available from http://www.e-flux.com/journal/the-obligation-to-self-design. [Accessed on 19/06/2014]

KLEIN, NAOMI. (2011) *No Logo: De strijd tegen de dwang van de wereldmerken (No Logo: Taking Aim at the Brand Bullies.* First edition published in 2000). Rotterdam: Lemniscaat.

LEHMANN, ULRICH (2009) Le mot dans la mode. In: Bra Jan. Teunissen, José. *Fas & Imagination.* ArtEZ Pres d'JongeHond.

LIPOVETSKY, GILLES. (2007) Moderne Luxe, Postmoderne Luxe. In: Brand, Jan Teunissen, José. *Mode & Accessoires.* Uitgeverij Te Lannoo bv.

LONDON, BERNARD. (1932) *Ending the Depression Tr Planned Obsolescence.* [Online] Available from ht www.r2launch.nl/index.php/lifetime/planned-obsolescence. [Accessed on 05/02/2014]

LOOS, ADOLF. (1908) *Orname and Crime.* [Online]. Avai ble from http://www2.gw edu/~art/Temporary_SL/1 pdfs/Loos.pdf. [Accessed 10/10/2007]

MARCHETTI, LUCA. (2009) F the Object to the Invisible tail Experience within Spa Fashion and Body. In: Bra Jan, Teunissen, José. *Fas & Imagination.* ArtEZ Pres d'JongeHond.

MAYNARD KEYNES, JOHN. (1 *Economic Possibilities for Grandchildren.* [Online] N York: W.W.Norton & Co.. able from http://www.eco yale.edu/smith/econ116a keynes1.pdf. [Accessed: 01/04/2014] (Scanned fr John Maynard Keynes, Es in Persuasion, New York: W.W.Norton & Co., 1963, 358-373.)

(2014) *Nike women's-only store with fitness studio opens in Newport Beach* [Online] 20/11/2014. Available from http://news.nike.com/news/new-nike-experience-store-in-newport-beach-california-combines-best-of-women-s-products-with-fitness-studio. [Accessed on 07/05/2015]

‹ARD, VANCE. (1960) *The Waste Makers*. United States: Vance Packard Inc. (first edition)

II, JOSEPH B. & GILMORE, JAMES H. (2011) *The Experience Economy*. Updated Edition. Boston: Harvard Business Review Press.

EDOUARD. *Modernity, Postmodernity, Hypermodernity* [Online] Available from http://www.counter-currents.com/2011/06/modernity-postmodernity-hypermodernity/ [Accessed on 14/01/2015]

:S MEYER, FRANZ. (2013) *Handbook of Ornament, 3003 Illustrations*. First edition: 1957. New York: Dover Publications.

H, DAVID. (2010) Is There a New Normal? *Fashion Journal 2009-2010, Fashion Performance Performing Fashion.* (2009-2010).

WSTUDIO (2014) *FOR FA$HION'S S@KE*. In conversation. [Online video]. 2014. Available from http://showstudio.com/project/in_conversation/for_fashions_sake. [Accessed on 25/07/ 2014]

MEL, GEORG (1904) *Fashion.* [Online] (09/2010). Available from http://sites.middlebury.edu/individualandthesociety/files/2010/09/Simmel.fashion.pdf [Accessed on 15/01/2015]

SIMON, JOSHUA. (2013) *Neomaterialism*, Berlin: Sternberg Press.

SKIDELSKY, ROBERT & SKIDELSKY, EDWARD. (2012) Hoeveel is Genoeg? Geld en het verlangen naar een goed leven. (*How Much is Enough? Money and the Good Life).* Amsterdam: De Bezige Bij.

SAUMAREZ SMITH, CHARLES. (1993) *The Rise of Design: Design and Domestic Interior in Eighteenth-Century England.* London: Pimlico.

TED. (2004) *What Consumers Want.* [Online video]. February 2004. Available from http://www.ted.com/talks/joseph_pine_on_what_consumers_want.html. [Accessed on 04/04/2014]

THOMAS, DANA. (2007) *Deluxe, How Luxury Lost its Lustre.* New York: Penguin Press.

WIGLEY, MARK. (2001) *White Walls, Designer Dresses. The Fashioning of Modern Architecture.* Cambridge / London: MIT Press.

WIKIPEDIA *The Experience Economy* [Online]. Available from http://en.wikipedia.org/wiki/The_Experience_Economy. [Accessed on 20/03/2014]

Fig 1: KRAYBILL, DONALD B. (2014) Slow Time is God's Time. *Vestoj, The journal of sartorial matters. On Slowness.* 5 (Autumn 2014) p. 45.

Fig 2: BARTLETT, DJURDJA. (2010) *Fashion East, The Spectre that Haunted Socialism.* Cambridge / London: The MIT Press. p. 5

Fig 3: BALLARD, J.G (1967) *The crystal world.* Berkley Medallion Edition. New York: Berkley Publishing Corporation. p. 74

Fig 4: MURAKAMI, HARUKI. (2005) *Kafka on the Shore.* London: Vintage. p. 560

Fig 6: WEILL, VALERIE & CHANCEL, PHILIPPE. (2004) *Paris in store.* London: Thames & Hudson Ltd, p. 128

Fig 7: MURAKAMI, HARUKI. (2005) *Kafka on the Shore.* London: Vintage. p. 350

Fig 8: SHULMAN, A (ed.) (May 2017) *Vogue.* Cover, Photo by Lachlan Bailey, Fashion Editor Clare Richardson. London: Condé Nast.

Fig 9: KENNETH, RICHARD. (2014) *The Best Fashion Ads of Fall 2014* [Online] Available from http://theimprint.theimpression.com/2014/07/25/the-best-fashion-ads-of-fall-2014/ [Accessed in April 2015] Hermès advertisement, fall/winter 2014

Fig 10: WE Fashion (December 2016) brand magazine. The Netherlands.

Fig 11: MURAKAMI, HARUKI. (2012) *1Q84.* London: Vintage. p. 165

Fig 12: THE NATIONAL GEOGRAPHIC MAGAZINE (1935) Petra, Ancient Caravan Stronghold. *The national Geographic Magazine.* Vol. LXVII, (No.2, Feb.) p. 136.

Fig 13: WINTOUR, A (ed.) (February 2017) *Vogue.* Photo by Peter Lindbergh. New York: Condé Nast.

Fig 14: MURAKAMI, HARUKI. (2005) *Kafka on the Shore.* London: Vintage. p. 357

Fig 15: THE NATIONAL GEOGRAPHIC MAGAZINE, Vol LXVII, No.2, Feb. 1953 p. 314

Fig 16: GORDON, BEVERLY, (2011) *Textiles The Whole Story.* London: Thames & Hudson. p. 30

Onomatopee 121

Fashioning Value –
Undressing Ornament

Author:
Femke de Vries

Text editing:
Ruby Hoette
Hanka van der Voet

Translation:
Nanne op 't Ende

Graphic design:
Hans Gremmen

Publisher:
Onomatopee

Printing:
Drukkerij Roelofs

Edition:
1200

ISBN:
978-94-91677-44-1

Many thanks for
your critical reading,
input and advice:
Nanne op 't Ende
Ruby Hoette
Maaike Lauwaert
José Teunissen
Hanka van der Voet

Many thanks for your
support, process and/or
contentwise:
Marinus Augustijn
Ada Bosman
Chet Bugter
Daniela Dossi
Maaike Feitsma
gerlach en koop
Conny Groenewegen
Bas van den Hurk
Elisa van Joolen
Freek Lomme
Joke Robaard
Agnes Scholte
Sarah Sixma
Remco Torenbosch
Sue-an van der Zijpp
and my dearest family

This book, and the
preceding research,
have been generously
supported by:
Kunstraad Groningen
LeoXIII Gastatelier
Onomatopee
Stimuleringsfonds
Creatieve Industrie

Published in 2015,
reprinted in 2017

www.femkedevries.com